I0406039

BARKING UP THE RIGHT TREE

A Groomer's Guide to Creating, Growing, and Maintaining a Profitable Business

By Kari Rouse

Barking Up The Right Tree

Cover designed by Kari & Matthew Rouse

Editing by Matthew Rouse

Back Cover Photo by Edina Clagett
v1.0

Kari Rouse
Visit my website at BarkCartons.com

Printed in the United States of America

First Printing: July 2019

ISBN- 9781075752964

By Kari Rouse

Table of Contents

By Kari Rouse

For Matt who dares to stand up and be a creative force in this world.

For all the late nights and early mornings.

You inspire me on a daily basis.

Without your love and support this book would still be rattling around in my mind.

Every day we're hustling.

By Kari Rouse

FOREWARD

By Matthew Rouse

Kari was putting in another 14 hours day.

I took an early lunch from my work to get us both some food and then Kari would take a break from the salon and we would sit on a bench near her grooming salon and eat and chat.

We had to eat fast. There were five Pomeranians coming in at 11:30 and they weren't going to bath themselves.

We planned to meet for dinner, but that also got pushed back because a dog pooped in a kennel while waiting for her Mom to pick her up. She had to be washed and blown out again.

It was 4th of July weekend this weekend and everyone wanted to get their dogs looking pretty before their BBQs and Family gatherings. Also, Kari was putting little red, white, and blue ribbons in all the dogs' hair.

I was used to it though.

Kari worked long hours because she was always booked solid.

She was booked out months in advance and any of the schedule that wasn't full was easily filled with all the referral clients.

She had to hand off the business to the other groomers at the shop because she could fit all the dogs into her schedule, working 60+ hour weeks.

Kari was able to do all this while also managing the shop, staff scheduling, product orders, answering the phones, reports, etc.

And this wasn't the first time. When she was successful at one shop, the company she worked for had asked if she could go help another grooming salon that was dying. Sales were non-existent, they couldn't keep staff or customers, and no one was happy. It was a disaster...

That is until Kari got there.

Within months the place was booming, they had to hire more staff, the phones had started to ring again. There was a buzz about the salon and people were leaving as happy customers with happy animals.

And she did it again at another salon, and again at another salon, each time turning them into happy profitable grooming shops.

Somehow, Kari and I still managed to get engaged during our short times together outside of our hectic schedules and now we have a cute house next to a community garden and raise our little 3-year-old daughter Faith Magnolia Rouse and hang out with our rescued Boston Terrier, Rosie.

Kari has retired from the salon business and now helps groom shop owners and managers learn the ropes of business and marketing with her company, Bark Cartons.

This book is the story of how you can turn your salon around. Or if you are a groomer working within a company, how you can grow your client base.

...and have a little fun learning about it at the same time.

It was Blaise Pascal who wrote back in 1657, "If I had more time, I would have written a shorter letter." He was speaking to the time it takes to edit something down to the most important bits.

Barking Up the Right Tree is just the important bits.

Everyone is busy these days and you need to be busy building your clientele, so this book is respectful of your time and gives you a few Yorkie sized stories and some Great Dane sized knowledge.

Take a walk with Kari down the path to profitability. *Fetch* a cup of your favorite warm beverage and *sit and stay* reading the whole book.

Once you've read it through, I recommend you go back with a pen and some sticky notes and make the notes of all the things you need to work on, and paste them on the pages you need to find again later.

If you act on those notes, you will soon find yourself wondering how you didn't always do things this way.

Not only will you grow as a person, and as a business leader, but this book will help you find the goldmine hidden in your salon.

By Kari Rouse

CHAPTER 1

Story

Teddy was one of the best Westie you could ask for with the softest fur around (so difficult to work with). Sadly, he passed away last year at the ripe old age of 17 years old.

Teddy was one of my many long-time clients. Every time I moved to a different shop, they followed. It didn't matter that for a year I moved to a salon that was a 50-minute drive away, or when I partially 'retired' from grooming to raise my daughter. Like clockwork, Teddy would show up on my table every 6-8 weeks.

Because of Teddy, I was introduced to a new family that I would have never met if they had not brought him into my shop that first time so many years ago. I watched their daughter grow into a lovely young girl and budding track star. We exchanged recipes, talked about our vacations, and even the struggles we were going through in life. I found that a groomers job is much like that of a hairdresser, or bartender, in that people will share stories of their lives with you. Some of which you may not want to hear. Over the years we became friends.

You don't become a groomer for the glamorous aspects of the job. In fact, you know it can be one of the messiest and grossest jobs around. Starting the day clean, and ending it covered in dirt, hair, dander, water, and potentially fleas or ticks. And I haven't even brought up the unmentionables of Poop Poop or Peep Peep as my 3-year old daughter calls it, Anal Glands, or other mystery bodily fluids.

Becoming a groomer isn't about playing with puppies all day either! Although I used to love/hate that comment from everyone who wasn't in the industry as to what you do with your time all day.

No, to be a successful groomer you need more than just skill and talent with scissors, more than your animal handling skills, more than being able to work well with coworkers, and more than time management skills.

Grooming is about building trust and creating relationships with clients. Building a relationship is stronger than any single shop, town, or company.

You become family.

If you are in this business for the long haul, you will see generations of animals from the same family. You will watch children grow up and go to college and see clients grow older and pass away. You will watch it all and be included in this precious gift, if you take the time with each client.

CHAPTER 2

Introduction

Like most groomers, growing up I never knew what I wanted to be. In school I got excellent grades, and when I graduated high school, I went to college. Not because I knew what I was doing, rather because that is just what you do (or so I thought).

I started off majoring in Anthropology but midway through my first year, I realized that I should probably major is something a bit more practical as well. So, I added a Business major to my course load. Upon graduating I still didn't know what I wanted to do. Instead of using my fancy new degrees, I thought that I might like to marry my love of animals with my new-found business knowledge and start a boarding kennel.

What better place to learn the business than to get a minimum wage job as a kennel attendant? (My parents weren't pleased with this decision.)

During my short stint in the kennel I learned so much about working with animals in a professional setting, and while I was there one of the groomers showed me the basics of how to groom dogs.

The problem was the money.

I wasn't going to be paying off my student debt with a minimum wage job and still be able to afford to live (or to save enough to open a business). One of my coworkers had quit the kennel to get a grooming job at one of those big box retail stores and was making what I thought at the time was a ton of cash. I decided to make the leap with her.

Quickly I moved up the ranks to Grooming Manager and was leading my own team. This married both my business skills and my innate ability to read and work with animals.

Over the years I lead the largest team in our district with the highest numbers, trained many other groomers, was sent to several stores in the region to train their Grooming Managers and staff, all while doing a bit of grooming on my own and helping a friend in her shop when I had days off.

I put my heart and soul into this profession for 15 years before I moved on. At about the halfway point in my career I seriously injured my back at work causing me to take more than a month off work and do some intensive rehab work.

The normal wear and tear on my body from a busy grooming schedule caused me to rethink what I was putting my body though. My fingers, wrists, forearms, shoulders, and back hurt on a daily basis.

At my peak I was grooming average of 8-10 dogs (or more) by myself during my shift. Often, I would put in extremely long hours grooming if someone called out sick. And let's not forget the mad rush of the holiday season!

With hard work and some business skills I was able to pay off my student debt, purchase my first brand new car, and buy my home.

YOU can do that too, if you implement the things from this book into your own business.

When I looked up the statistics of what an average groomer makes in the United States I was floored.

Depending on the website that you look at the range was anywhere between $19k and $35k. I'm not sure if these data points include tips, but that is way too low!

I am going to show you how you can be a Groomer, doing something you love, and make a good living.

Grooming is a highly skilled profession as well as heavy physical labor. I don't know about you, but I definitely wouldn't be doing everything that this job entails and be happy with the above stated paycheck at the end of the week. If this is where you are at right now, that is a good starting point, but with the addition of implementing the tips in this book you will see your wages increase on a daily and weekly basis.

You can be an employee or grooming manager for a big box company, a groomer in a small shop, a mobile groomer, or own your own salon.

The key is that you think of yourself as your own business.

You need to make relationships with clients so that they come back to YOU, not the person using the table next to you, or the salon down the street.

If you are happy with whatever walks in your door and don't want to put in any extra time or money into building your grooming empire, you can set this book aside and continue fighting for the table scraps cast aside from the leaders in your salon. I don't mean to sound harsh, but building a booming business takes some planning, implementation, and hustle in order for you to see it pay off in the end.

If it was easy, everyone else would already be doing it.

CHAPTER 3

Theory

Let me take a moment to discuss some basic marketing theory. I will be using these concepts throughout the book but want to give you a baseline to go from. When you build a strategy from the theory and tactics in this book, you can achieve extraordinary results.

Let's start with what I would consider the Basic Level of Service. This is the bar you must reach to be considered a real business. If your standards are not reaching this minimum level of service, you have work to do.

Every customer who walks into your door has a few immediate expectations. The shop looking presentable, the employees to have a basic level of good customer service, the dogs to be treated well, and when they pick up their dog, they expect them to be clean, smelling good, and have a decent haircut that looks like what you talked about at check-in.

For the most part, the haircut doesn't have to be perfect either. Don't get me wrong, the more skilled you are at grooming, the easier it is to establish and maintain a regular clientele, but that is not necessary on its own. It is the relationship you build with each client that will keep your clients coming back.

Over the years I mentored several apprentices in the art of grooming. For most people it doesn't come naturally. It takes practice. You need an artistic eye to see the sculpture under that block of clay (or under all the dirt and matting). Understanding how hair flows and how to work with different hair types can be challenging. On top of all that you NEED the innate ability to read dog behavior.

This is a trade where it all gets better with experience.

I had a schnauzer on my table getting finished one bright sunny afternoon when another client came in with their dog ready to be dropped off. They happened to enter right when I was trimming the last eyebrow. To my horror Lucy, the schnauzer, perked her brow at the exact moment I closed my scissors and in slow motion I witnessed her beautiful hair floating down to rest on the table...

At that point there was nothing that I could do because you can't glue hair back on. Instead I had to break the news to Alice, her owner, that she had one short brow.

Because I had forged a relationship with Alice over the years of grooming Lucy, she wasn't upset at all and simply stated that "hair grows back", she paid her bill without complaint, handed me a tip, and said she would see me in 6 weeks at her next appointment.

Another day in my salon I had 4 students and was going over the standard for the various poodle haircuts. One of my coworkers had a Mini Poodle on her table and I pointed to her feet.

"Take a look at this dog. Obviously, her owner has asked to have her clean feet go up higher. See how it looks like she has a pair of highwater pants on? The line should be where the crease in her ankle is. Do you see how the bend clearly separates the foot from the leg here? This owner has obviously asked for the line to be higher for some reason. Maybe they go to the dog park where there is a lot of mud, or the beach, and it is easier to keep the feet clean, or they just like it higher."

I went on to explain other parts of the dogs' anatomy, where the hips are, neckline, etc., and how to hide flaws in the dogs' build with different haircuts. Later in the day my experienced groomer who had the poodle on her table came up to me in private to ask a question.

"When you pointed out the clean feet on my poodle to your students, were you serious that my line should have been lower?"

"Yes," I said. "Why?"

"Because I have always made my line that high, and none of my customers have ever said anything to me." she stated.

This groomer had clearly built relationships with her clients and when they wanted the 'standard' poodle-cut they now expected the clean feet to be higher.

I don't want to get into an argument here. A standard haircut is a standard for a reason. The AKC has designated standard haircuts for the show ring to highlight the 'perfect' specimen. Most of us, however, are not show groomers.

I often explained to clients and to my students that each groomer has their own style. Think of it being similar to handwriting. Each person's handwriting differs, so how can we expect each person to scissor a dog's hair exactly the same?

What if the original groomer is sick one day and another has to cover for her? A good groomer may be able to perform the same groom and mimic those highwater poodle feet, but they won't have the same relationship with the client as the original groomer. That relationship is forged over time, through phone calls, check-ins, check-outs, a mutual love for their animal, and so on.

Creating these relationships with your clients is key to growing and maintaining a thriving grooming business.

Client Lifetime Value

Depending on where you live prices will differ, but let's just use $50 as an average groom price to keep the math simple. Let's also assume that your average client comes in every 6 weeks to get groomed.

When talking about the average client you can expect them to keep coming back year after year until they move out of town, the animal or the human passes away, or you don't meet their expectations in some way and they move on to a different groomer. For this example, let's also assume our average customer stays with you for 3 years.

Every six weeks is roughly 9 grooms per year.

That's 27 grooms in 3 years.

At $50 per groom, that is $1350 in revenue from that customer.

This is the Customer Lifetime Value (CLV). $1350.

When you make decisions about your marketing in the future, you should be making those decisions based on a customer bringing in $1350 of revenue, not just the $50 you get on their first visit. This simple theory is how some businesses grow and some stagnate or go out of business. This is how you should start thinking about your business long-term.

I will talk later about adding extra service options for clients as a way to give yourself a raise and make more money per client. This way you don't have to take extra dogs to make more money, simply sell an add on service.

Creating Memorable Moments

A Memorable Moment is the next key theory we need to be clear with. A Memorable Moment happens when you personalize the service to each customer.

Remembering the customers' name and dog's name when they enter the door. Sending a get-well card to the owner's home when they, or a family member, or the dog is sick. Asking them how their Family Vacation to Disney Land was at their next visit. It is something specific to each customer that shows you care about them.

Creating these special moments does not have to take a lot of time, or money.

You are not Oprah, you don't have to give a car away with every groom. I will go over more examples of Memorable Moments in later chapters.

Follow-up

Follow-up is another key tool in building great customer relationships and a clientele who are repeat customers.

What is follow-up?

Follow-up can be many things, or just a few things. The key is to be consistent, make it something that is repeatable, and it can't cost you so much money or time that makes it difficult to keep up.

One idea for Follow-up is to simply call your client who had their appointment this week and ask, "How Benji is doing?"

Ask how the customer likes the haircut, or if they want you to note a change for next groom. This way it is easier to put in your grooming notes the changes for the next haircut rather than trying to remember back 6 or 8 weeks on how short to cut the dog's beard.

Another idea is to take a picture of each groom dog you do and send the customer a card with their own dog's picture.

You will remember the haircut by having a picture to reference, your client will get a great card with a photo of their dog, they will want to share the card with their neighbors and friends, and they will have your contact information handy for the next time they need to call you.

One service that makes this easy is called Send Out Cards. I will go over it in more detail later in the book.

The most important follow-up you can do is to call your clients to remind them of their pre-booked appointments. Chapter 6 goes over all the details about Pre-booking clients and more on follow-up. For now, it is just important to note that follow-up keeps you top of mind with your clients.

Talk Triggers and Remarkable Content

These are fancy terms for getting people talking about you and your business.

In the example above, the personalized card with a photo of the client's pet after their groom is a Talk Trigger. That owner is going to show off that card to their friends and family and keep it on the shelf to look at.

It Triggers a discussion.

Remarkable Content primarily focuses on Social Media Content and website content but can be in the physical world as well. This concept is not referring to Content that is Remarkable, but instead focuses of Content that people make a Remark about.

In Seth Godin's book Purple Cow, he goes into further detail about Remarkable Content. The idea is that if you saw a Purple cow on the side of the road you would make a Remark to someone about it.

Fitting in with all the other grooming shops is suicide for your business. It's a crowded marketplace and everyone is trying to get more business, but you do it by being different. Remarkable Content is how you show your unique talent and style.

The Pray Method vs. The Strategic Marketing and Implementation Method

There are two methods to getting New Clients. The Pray method vs. The Strategic Marketing and Implementation Method. Pray Method consists of you sitting back in your salon waiting for someone to call you and Praying that someone walks through your door.

Not a good way to run or grow your business...

When your business implements the Strategic Marketing and Implementation Method tools outlined in this book the end goal is to create an unpaid army of Brand Ambassadors (Your clients) who go out and tell all their friends and family about how awesome you are!

You will start to get Referral Clients walking in your door and calling out of the blue who already love you, without you having to find them and WOW them yourself. Another key benefit of Referral Clients is that they are 80% happier with your services (over random clients walking through your door) and more willing to Refer others to you.

That is a Win-Win in my book!

Target Market

When you start your business adventure, you need to clearly define who your Target Market is.

No, it isn't everyone who owns a dog.

Not everyone brings their dogs in for grooming, some view it as a basic service, some view it as a luxury item, some view it as an emergency service ("Hello, my dog has been skunked..."), and some are your regular every 4-8 week clients.

Going to the next step of defining your Target Market, you need to know who you are going to target as your regular (4-8 week repeats) clients. I have even had clients set up an every other week schedule. Bath only at the beginning of the month, and haircut 2 weeks later mid-month. These are amazing clients to have!

Remember there will always be a few outliers who come in for that 2x per year groom, out of towners, or skunked emergency services. The people you are targeting are those who will come in on a regular basis. They are your bread and butter.

They pay your bills.

They become part of your family.

Your end goal is to build your business in such a way that you only have time for your scheduled regular clients. The outliers like 'emergency' and 'once-a-year' dogs are an unknown when it comes to condition, temperament, and time needed to complete the groom. Once established you can send those ‘unknowns’ down the street.

“Ain’t nobody got time for that.”

Choosing a Target demographic depends on the individual groomer. Real Estate agents are in the same boat.

Not every client makes a perfect match. That is why they have specialties and look for specific types of people to work with. One might specialize in the high-end neighborhood on the lake, another will go after all the country homes with property, while the next looks to only do investment properties. They may take on an outlier, but for the most part they will refer that client out (they still get a small percentage of the commission when they refer out a deal).

Look at who you are currently attracting. Do you have a grooming specialty? Are you known as the best Poodle Groomer in town? Do you enjoy working with Terriers?

Another way to narrow it down is if you enjoy working with a specific type of people, for example, are you an active member of a minority community, a member of a local Church, or do you have a hobby that can attract like-minded clients?

There are so many ways you can narrow it down. You will read about another example in the next chapter as well.

Customer Avatar

A Customer Avatar is a fictional client that you create who is representative of your ideal client. If you serve multiple types of clients, you should be creating a Customer Avatar for each type of client.

You want to know more about them than just their basic demographics such as age and gender. You want to know what their hopes and dreams are. Where do they shop. What do they read? What do they watch? What are their problems/fears? Where do they get their information? What are their hobbies?

It is a good idea to list the common objections and questions you get from your current clients, so you can address them up front in your marketing and social media.

"But my last groomer was $20 cheaper?!?"

"It sounds like you were getting a great deal at your last grooming salon. My prices are based on my experience and talent. I also take into account my overhead to run this business, like shampoo costs, rent, and equipment upkeep..."

The more detailed you get in this step, the better you can focus your marketing toward them, and address their needs specifically.

See the appendix for a *Customer Avatar Worksheet* you can fill out.

By Kari Rouse

CHAPTER 4

Presentation

The first thing a customer sees when they enter your salon can make or break the experience.

I know what you're saying, "But we cut hair for a living, there is going to be some hair on the floor."

True, but if you clean up after every dog you groom the shop will look well maintained and sanitary. At some point there are going to be regulations set by the government for sanitation and safety.

You can read more about it, and get involved here: https://petgroomersandstylists.org/

Imagine going into a human hair salon and seeing piles of hair on the floor from multiple people. Would you want to get your hair cut there? I know I wouldn't.

People make assumptions, and the assumption they will make is that if you don't clean up the shop floor, you won't clean other things, or take care and attention with their beloved pet.

Besides hair on the floor you will want to keep your tools and other clutter organized and to a minimum. The desk should be clear of paperwork and items with client names should not be in plain view.

"How you do anything is how you do everything." How you handle the small things tells others how you handle other tasks.

You want people to know you are professional in everything you do.

Smell

The smell is a tough one. When you get a dirty dog wet, you automatically end up with that lovely wet dog smell.

The best way to make sure your shop is not plagued with a funky smell that lingers is to maintain a strict cleaning schedule. I had daily, weekly, and monthly cleaning duties and made sure those were done so that hair, dander, and dirt didn't sit around.

Using a scented shampoo and conditioner can go a long way to helping alleviate that smell, but what I found is I just did my best by using an air freshener. I like to use an essential oil spray with lavender in it, that way it smells nice, and has a calming effect for the dogs and yourself.

Appearance

In the first Chapter I mentioned starting the day clean and ending it dirty. When it comes to your appearance Groomers come in all sizes and shapes, tattoos or no, have various hair colors, and being an artistic bunch, you all have different styles of dress outside of work.

As a professional, how you appear to others matters and we already know that people are making assumptions in a split second when they walk into your shop.

What to Wear

Wear closed toe and skid resistant shoes (for safety), fast-drying pants and your Grooming Smock or apron. This is your daily uniform.

You are working with water, slick floors and fast-moving dogs. Safety is key when it comes to getting dressed for the grooming salon.

What Not to Wear

I have seen groomers wearing dresses and flip flops, or short shorts (that don't cover everything), and even full on Halloween costumes. Lawyers don't show up in the court room wearing a Hawaiian shirt and board shorts. You are a professional, dress appropriately.

I outlined Target Market last Chapter, but let's define it a bit further here. Know who you want to work with on a regular basis. Your Target Market (or regular clientele) will be the ones you keep on a schedule. They will come in every 4-8 weeks like clockwork. These customers are the ones who pay your bills.

You will also have some outliers. Some who call in an emergency, if they are driving through town on vacation, or who only come once or twice per year. I do not consider these your *target market.* I like to think of these customers as bonus customers.

The goal is to grow your business so that you are busy and booked out with your regular clients so that you don't have to take those wild card dogs.

I had one potential new customer call our Big Box Grooming Salon to schedule her appointment. One of my Groomers was scheduled to take care of this particular little poodle. My co-worker was wearing professional attire, but her hair was dyed a crazy color, she had on dark gothic like make-up, and has tattoos up and down her arms.

When she walked up to the desk to greet this client, the poodle lady took one look at her, turned around and never came back.

In this example the customer's expectations were not in line with what she was presented when she walked in.

Sometimes customers make assumptions and pre-judge you based on looks, just like the example of all the hair on the floor in your shop. She had no idea how sweet my coworker was, or how skilled she was at grooming, or how much she adored grooming poodles. You have a bit less leeway in a Corporate setting, but you still have the opportunity to attract the customers you want to work with.

If you want to be known as the best tattooed groomer on the West Coast, then you need to own it. Have pictures of yourself showing off your tattoos and holding a poodle on your website, social media, marketing...everywhere. You will naturally attract people who come to you because they identify with YOU.

Realize though, that you have also alienated another segment of the population who is NOT looking for that. You probably won't get a ton of Church ladies with their Teacup Yorkies coming in to see you.

And that's a good thing.

You want to have what is called "market fit" with your customers. You want them to have something in common with you and their peer group will also. That means they can refer their friends, who also like things you like.

Choose what works for you and your situation.

Once you choose your Target Market, go all in!

Attitude

Finally, I want to address your attitude. Every day is not perfect, some days are better than others. But even though you just got done re-bathing your finished dog because he pooped all over the kennel when you put him away, doesn't mean that when you walk out of your back room to greet a customer you should do so grumpily.

Always, and I mean ALWAYS greet each and every customer who walk through the door as if you have it all under control and you are having the most perfect day.

I know you are not a robot, and we all have emotions, but look at it from the customer's perspective.

They walk in to drop off their dog (or pick up, or ask a question), and you come out of the back pissed off and complaining about someone else's dog. That gives them the impression that you don't enjoy what you are doing, or you may not treat their dog with the utmost care and respect, or that maybe today isn't the right day to spend money with you.

On the other hand, let's say you just finish up re-bathing that same dog. Come out of the back of the salon and greet that same customer with a big smile on your face. Then ask them how you can help them today? You will find this second scenario will land you more repeat business in the long run.

I'm not saying that you shouldn't ever talk to your customers about the down parts of your day. What I am saying however, is that only those long-term customers who see you on a regular basis and have already established trust with you will be able to empathize with you.

As the saying goes, "you get more bees with honey!"

A Note for Owners and Managers

Gary Vaynerchuk is the CEO of VaynerMedia and is a huge player in the Digital Marketing landscape and has created a corporate culture of positivity.

He knows that in order to get the maximum productivity and quality out of your employees you must be invested in them.

Here are some general rules to follow to invest in your people.

1. **Give respect to get respect.**

If you want to attract the highest quality employees and retain them for the long term, you need to show them that you care about them. Show them that they are valued and respected.

It shows when you don't genuinely care about the well-being of your employees both inside and outside of your business. You start to create a culture of negativity in your business that leads to the loss of respect in the leadership of your business.

2. Understand what motivates your employees.

Over the years I learned that different things motivated different employees. To my surprise I learned that some/most employees are NOT motivated by money.

You need to understand that each person is unique and has their own goals and motivations in life. Find out what that is and use it. They may be motivated by money, recognition, coffee, food, etc.

Use positive reinforcement to recognize when your employees are excelling at their jobs. It shows them you care about them as a player on your team.

This understanding is a key part to great leadership. Using positive reinforcement helps to motivate and recognize your employees. Using personalized reinforcement shows that you value them and their contributions as a team player.

3. Be action oriented.

When you are the owner of the business or the manager, your employees look to you to set precedence. You need to model the behavior you want your employees to mirror.

You have heard the adage; *actions speak louder than words.*

Build your company culture through your actions.

Working next to your employees in the trenches on busy days creates an overall culture of positivity and connectivity. You are all on the same ship, you will sink or swim together.

4. Reward performance; don't play favorites.

Hard work should always be rewarded. On the flip side of that coin, if someone messes up, you should ALWAYS correct the problem immediately. Letting things slide creates tension and uncertainty in the workplace.

Over the years I have worked with several people who caused issues in the salon. Some didn't follow the rules, some were downright disrespectful of others, and some just kept messing up haircuts/or had poor customer service.

Not taking care of these issues when they happen creates unneeded tension, leads to issues with other employees, and can start to be a problem on the customer facing side of the business.

The discipline should be different depending on each situation.

Customer service skills and grooming skills can be improved with additional training. Rule infraction issues most of the time can be taken care of with a sit-down talk and refreshing their memory on expectations.

Blatant disrespect and dangerous behaviors should be taken care of immediately. I am by no means a lawyer and cannot advise you about firing an employee. However, certain things left to run their course without intervention can ruin your positive business culture, interfere with your positive interactions with clients, and eventually be the downfall of your business.

"I attract a crowd, not because I'm an extrovert or I'm over the top or I'm oozing with charisma. It's because I care." – ***Gary Vaynerchuk***

Gary cares deeply about his employees and the culture he is building in his business. He builds positivity and teamwork and doesn't tolerate negativity.

He knows positivity will attract a higher caliber employee who is more productive and fulfilled.

This personalized connection with your employees extends to your customers as well. Learn more about Personalized service for your clients in the next chapter.

By Kari Rouse

CHAPTER 5

Personalized Service for Clients

Just after my daughter turned One year old, we decided to take her to one of those cute kid haircut places where they sit in the little car and watch cartoons while they get their hair trimmed.

When we walked through the door there were no other kids in the salon. One of the stylists told us to pick whatever chair we wanted.

After choosing the fire truck and getting her sitting up there all belted in the stylist came over and asked what kind of haircut we were looking for. I explained that I wanted some bangs cut (her hair was always in her face), and just a slight trim. For the next 15 minutes she cut my daughter's hair, asked us if that is all and told us to go pay at the desk. She also said to pick a toy out of the chest by the register. That was it.

I was completely disappointed in the clinical approach and feel of the whole encounter.

She wasn't excited, she barely smiled, she didn't ask if this was my daughter's first haircut, she didn't lead us over to the register and show my daughter the toys that she could choose from in the chest.

It wasn't a warm experience.

Every client wants to think that they are your favorite client and you will bend over backwards to serve their every need. You don't have to bend over backwards, they just have to FEEL like you are. It is about making each customer feel special.

Unlike the lack-luster hair cutting lady, who more or less ruined the only first hair cut my daughter will ever have, I wanted to make sure every experience in my salon was the best it could be. I greeted every dog walking into my salon with more warmth and caring. I treated every animal with enthusiasm and excitement.

I expected more for a $30 haircut that took 15 minutes. We never went back, we didn't tip like we would have if the experience was more welcoming, and we didn't refer any new clients to them. In fact, we told everyone we knew how mediocre our experience was and to not go there.

This story could have been in the previous chapter about attitude, but I am including it here because it is important to understand how your customer service at check in and check out can have such huge effects on your business, retain more clients, lead to larger tips, and create more referral business.

This is the first and last impression for your customers.

Make it count.

My biggest pet peeve, pun intended, in the grooming industry is when a groomer states that they are in this profession because they don't like people and would rather work with dogs all day long.

Wake up!

Dogs don't drive themselves to your salon, and dogs don't pay your bills. If you want to build a large client base who come to their appointments like clockwork, refer their friends and family to you, and think of you like family you MUST cater to their needs and impress them with your outstanding customer service.

Check-in Procedure

This always includes a warm smile and exuberant greeting. "Hello Debbie! How is your day going today?"

Go AROUND the counter, drop to the dog's level and greet the dog with pets and play.

"HI Buffy!!! I have missed you so much since the last time you were in. How are you sweet girl??? Oh, you are such a good girl!..."

At this time, you should be checking the dog's skin and coat. Their ears, feet, tail, eyes, and nose for any signs of skin issues, bugs, wounds, sensitivities, matting...

Once you have all this information you can start your check-in with the Pet Parent as to the services that Buffy needs done today. Point out the skin flakes and tell them about the great conditioner that you have to help moisturize the skin, or the nail Dremel service you can do to get those nails as short as possible and that is a smooth finish so they don't scratch up the owners' legs when they jump.

You should also discuss the hair cut details and any other health issues or concerns you see.

My employees always teased me about my phone voice and how I could go from speaking very plainly to them to plastering a smile on my face and greeting my customers like a drag car going from 0 to 60 in 2.5 seconds.

People can hear a smile over the phone. Trust me.

Check-in is the most important customer interaction because it sets the tone for everything to follow.

It shows you care about that dog and that customer. That you have solutions to their problems, and that you are confident in your skills to accomplish what they are asking you to do.

If you work for a corporation, you will be familiar with this as their 'upselling' procedure, but it is more than that. It is more than the company's bottom line. It is more than simply making more money.

You are taking care of the animal's needs.

More importantly you are making a connection with each customer when you use this check-in procedure.

Let's take shampoo for example.

If Buffy has flakey and scaly skin you could just us a basic shampoo to get the dog's fur 'clean', but that isn't going to do anything to soothe or help remedy the skin problem. You have shampoo specifically for this issue and know that following it up with a conditioner will help soothe the skin even further. Using those products costs more than just using your basic shampoo, so you should charge the customer extra for those.

As a side note, it is also good to ask what food they are feeding their dog as it is probably a food related issue causing the dog's skin to look like that. You may be able to recommend a food that will help clear up the issue from the inside.

Don't lose money, get paid more for using more expensive products. Even though you are essentially doing the same amount of work. This is the easiest way to give yourself a raise WITHOUT grooming more dogs on a daily basis.

This is the same for human shampoo products. If someone has dandruff, using a bottom shelf, cheap shampoo won't solve the problem. But if you pay a little extra and get the Jasön Dandruff Shampoo plus Conditioner, you will see your scalp heal and you won't have flakes dropping on your shoulders anymore. Trust me, my husband uses this shampoo after trying everything on the market and it is AMAZING!

In fact, I said the same to a Massage Therapist in one of my networking groups who adds in aromatherapy, hot stones and cupping to her regular 60-minute massage without a price increase.

She spent more money and time getting trained in those modalities, and she had to purchase extra tools. These should be used as additions to her business to help her stand out from the crowd. A way to customize and increase the value of her services offered.

When businesspeople regularly throw these extra services in without charging any extra, it makes me think they are not confident in their services and are trying to compensate with freebies.

Start Building a Relationship

At check-in, when talking to your return clients you will also use this time to build a relationship. Ask about their children, significant other, the vacation they just got back from, how their holiday went, what hobbies they have. Get to know them.

I had a client with a Rat Terrier bring her dog in every 8 weeks for a bath. In truth anyone in my salon could have done that dog. But I made the relationship with her.

One day I asked her what she was going to do when Missy was getting her bath. She said she was going to work on finishing the final draft of her book that she was writing. I asked her about it briefly and she went on her way.

The next time she came for a bath I asked her how her edits were going and if she was finished. She was floored that I remembered.

I said, "Of course I remember. I would also like to purchase a copy of the book when it gets printed if you have an extra."

It was a family memoir she wrote for her Grandchildren, so they would always remember the adventures she had in Europe during the War and beyond.

When the book was published, she gave me a signed copy with a hand-written note in it. What a special gift to receive. This created a Memorable Moment between this client and me. From that time on, she never went to another groomer.

Using this personalized check-in process with EVERY client and potential client will automatically lead to repeat business.

Your clients will wait for you to get back from vacation, won't settle for getting a groom from the person standing at the table next to you, or down the street when you are booked, and will come in more often because of the relationship you have formed with them.

No matter what services and products another grooming shop offers, the thing they can't compete with is your relationship. If you have the relationship, your customers won't leave, they will tip more, and complain less.

By Kari Rouse

CHAPTER 6

Pre-booking Clients and Follow-up

Keep a record of your clients. It doesn't really matter how you do it. It can be as simple as writing them down on a piece of paper, keeping them organized in an excel spreadsheet, or entering them into a Customer Relationship Management system (CRM) like Send Out Cards.

The point is, you need to know who your clients are, at what frequency they are coming in, and any additional data you need to remember, such as family names, vacations they are going on, hobbies they may have, etc. I had a pretty good memory when it came to that stuff, but when you start getting into the 100's of clients it can be difficult to keep them all separate in your head. And you don't want to ask the wrong client the wrong thing.

If you are a numbers' person, we can look at it this way. If you groom 5 dogs a day, work 5 days a week, and all your clients are on a 6-week rotation you are looking at having 150 regular clients. 5*5*6=150. I was grooming 8 dogs 5 days a week. Now we are looking at 240 regular clients, or 8*5*6=240. That's a lot of people to remember things about!

This can vary a lot when it comes to how often your average client visits your salon. Some of mine came every 4 weeks, while others came every 8 weeks (most were every 6 weeks). I also had a few outliers who traveled in from out of town every 12 weeks, and a few who came in twice per year. But you get the point.

Pre-booking Clients

Let's talk about pre-booking your clients. If you currently don't pre-book out your clients, it is going to take a bit of time to train them to this new way of doing things.

And, it's easier to train your clients than it is to train your dog!

At first, they are going to tell you they don't know what their schedule will be in 6 or 8 weeks. They will resist. But remember, you are running a successful and busy grooming schedule (even if you are slow now, once you put all these tips in place you WILL be busy).

You want to make sure that when it is time for that dog to come back in for their next appointment that you have time in your schedule, and the best way to do that is by booking it in advance. I always let them know that I would call them a week in advance to remind them, and we could always move it around if needed.

Here is an example:

You: "Fluffy is ready to go Mrs. Jones. We should book your next appointment to keep him looking great."

Mrs. Jones: "I will just call when he needs a bath again."

You: "I know it seems more convenient to do it that way, but we are already booking up fast and I want to make sure you can still get Fluffy in to see me. Don't worry, we'll put it on the books and then I'll call you a week before and we can adjust the date and time if you can't make it then."

Mrs. Jones: "Ok, that's probably a good idea."

At the height of my career I was grooming between 7-10 dogs a day. These were busy days. I worked Tuesday thru Saturday and on top of my full schedule of dogs I had all my manager tasks to complete as well, scheduling employees, staying on budget, watching our salon numbers, ordering supplies, handling complaints, follow-up with customers, walk-in nail trims, and fielding questions from staff, management, and potential clients.

There was no time to squander.

Setting up a schedule is the first step in this very important system. I call it the BARC system. Book-Appointment-Rebook-Call - the BARC booking system. Using this acronym is an easy way to remember the steps needed in this pre-booking process.

Each week I would look ahead at my schedule, keeping in mind my daily and weekly tasks that I needed to accomplish as well. When you set yourself up with Daily and Weekly tasks in a checkbox system you won't forget anything and you will get more accomplished overall.

I still keep a weekly calendar for all my work and personal things needing done.

Yours may look something like this:

Daily

Check payroll from previous week and daily

Look at the schedule for the day

Check your supplies and add to the supply list as you are running low

Clean as you go

Make reminder calls

Groom dogs

Etc...

Weekly

Order supplies needed

Complete weekly cleaning duties (have a separate list of Daily/Weekly/Monthly cleaning tasks)

Create a schedule for staff.

I found it is easier to have set schedules for your employees. This way you allow for ease with pre-booking. Your staff automatically knows when they are working in 6-8 weeks. (if you have staff)

Make your reminder calls for the next week

Etc...

You will know what works in your business. The point of a list is to be able to go on auto-pilot and still maintain consistency even when you are tired after a long day/week.

Schedule Your Day Appropriately

I groomed my dogs in batches, taking them in every half hour for the first couple of hours. I would bathe and dry, bathe and dry, bathe and dry, bathe and dry, then finish, finish, finish, finish. Usually I would have a chance to grab my lunch or a snack before my next round would come in, but sometimes it would be crammed between dogs somewhere.

There are many different ways to organize your grooming schedule.

Some groomers have the dogs all come in the morning at the beginning of the day and they will call pet parents as they get done. Some will take a group of dogs in the morning and then a group of dogs in the afternoon. While other groomers take 2 at a time every couple hours or so and rotate through them.

There is no 'Right' way to do it. Experiment with it and find what works best for you, your style, and speed. Once you find what works, stick to it.

When each and every dog was being picked up, I would point out that I had pre-booked that dog in 4, 6, 8 weeks (depending on the frequency that owner liked). Let them know that I would call and confirm their appointment the week before, and that we could change it if needed.

Remember, you are training the owner. This is how you pay your own bills on time and know that you will always have money coming in next week, next month, next year.

One word of warning. If you do not call to remind your clients, you will look like you have a full schedule, and then have NOBODY show up! This can make or break your business. I can't stress this enough. You HAVE to follow up with your clients!

Self-Care

Let's take a break for a few minutes to talk about self-care.

Briefly I want to mention that you should make sure to take care of yourself and your needs throughout the day. If you need to stop and take a break, do so, it is better for you and the dogs if you are not having a blood sugar crash in the middle of grooming a dog.

Remember to drink plenty of water.

Take vacations!

One or two real vacations a year are a MUST to avoid groomer fatigue and burnout.

I liked to split my time up and take one after the holiday rush in January. It tends to be a slower time because you just had most of your clients in during the crazy holiday time, and the winter weather can get you down (depending on where you live).

I also took a short break during the summer months. Splitting your vacations up so they are about 6 months apart will give you something to look forward to and help reduce the likelihood of burnout.

I know what you are saying...

If I don't work, I don't make money. This topic could be a whole book in itself. Sit down and really look at your finances. What are you spending money on, how much are you saving, where are you wasting money? Create a plan to set aside money specifically for your vacations.

Once you have your BARC tool in place and working, you will have a steady flow of income. Make sure your money is working

FOR you, not the other way around. Sit down with a Financial Advisor to get a fresh set of eyes on your finances. This is usually a free service. You only start paying them when you have them manage your money and investments.

I usually made the most money before and after my vacations (not including busy holiday times). When you know when you are going to go on vacation or take a day off for a doctor's appointment, you can book around those times instead of having to call 30 clients to move them to another week right before you go out of town. This allows you to book heavier before and after your vacations to make up the money you are not making the week you are gone.

Keep a list of clients who call in to cancel their appointments, or who can't come in due to illness. This will allow you to reach out to them with options to fill your slow days. Try to book them right away or write down what day you will call them back. Clients won't fall through the cracks this way. They are more likely to book with you, not your co-worker, and the sooner you can get them in, that leaves time for those last-minute call-in or walk-in clients.

Customer Communication

Managing communication with your clients is vital to your business. Making sure you greet them appropriately, manage expectations, pre-book, call to remind for appointments, and follow up, will ensure you have a thriving business.

Send Out Cards is a great marketing resource that helps to create those client relationships. As I mentioned previously it has a CRM system as one of the features. You can add client names, addresses, phone numbers, birthdays, kids' names, dog names, add a list of clients they have referred to you, where they went on vacation. The list is infinite on how you can use this tool and what you can keep track of.

The main feature of this service is that you can create single cards, or card campaigns (sending the same card to multiple people on a list) to send to your clients. Whether it be a pre-made card, or a card that you can drag and drop photos onto, you can then personalize with your own message inside and your business information on the back. The company will print it, stuff it, and send it for you. Saving you time and money.

Whatever way you manage your client contact for follow-up in your business, keep in mind to make Memorable Moments along the way.

I will go over more examples of Follow-up in the next Chapter about Memorable Moments as well as Chapter 11, Marketing.

CHAPTER 7

Memorable Moments

In my state, Oregon, there is a huge rivalry between the Ducks and Beavers College Football teams. You are either a Duck, or a Beaver. Whether you grew up in a sport loving family, if you went to school at one of these two colleges, or you have jumped on the bandwagon because your friends are fans.

In almost every town or state, there is a rivalry of popular sports teams, or other things, like types of Pizza, or the best ______ in town. The point is, if your customers are crazy about a rivalry, use it!

In Oregon, people sport either Green and Yellow for University of Oregon, or Black and Orange, for Oregon State University. You see car flags, banners, people in their team colors, and bumper stickers, the whole state is sporting their teams' colors.

Once a year, the two rival teams play one another in what is called "the Civil War Game". I went to the local craft store, purchased a bunch of fabric and made Bandanas for all the dogs going through my shop. During check-in I mentioned that we had a special going on and if they purchased the Add-on package (fancy shampoo, conditioner, and toothbrushing) they could choose their team and Fido would go out sporting the corresponding bandana.

It was a huge hit!

We had a fun rivalry going in our salon with each stylist wearing their team's colors, our customers upgraded their services to get the bandana, the dogs went out looking stylish, we made more money, and most importantly our customers told their friends and family. It was a Remarkable Moment.

A Remarkable Moment is a moment that stands out as being positive, memorable, and unique. It is a moment someone will "make a remark about" to someone else they know (or everyone they know!). And often people will take photos and share them online, further expanding the reach of your Remarkable Moment.

This promotion was also a Memorable Moment. Every year afterwards our clients looked forward to 'Civil War' in the grooming salon, but more importantly we had another connection with them.

**Make a note in your CRM system what team they root for so you can remember it in the future.*

Most of the college football games were held on Saturdays. During the season we could talk about how their team was doing or ask the score on game days (I worked on Saturday's and wasn't able to go to many games, but this created another connection with my clients).

When we create Memorable Moments, we can note that information about our customer and then the following year, we can let those customers know we're going to do the same things again this year! This can help drive sales, and get your customers to spread the word of your promotion for you.

In general, finishing touches like bows and bandanas go a long way to adding an extra something special to your grooms without breaking the bank. I liked to have some basic bandana and bow options and change them out depending on which holiday was coming up. For example, Red, White, and Blue for the 4th of July.

Remember when it comes to religious holidays, you will need to be sensitive of people's beliefs. Asking if someone wants Red and Green ribbons in December is different than asking if they want Christmas ribbons. You'll have to know your customers and try to be sensitive, so you don't offend anyone.

I had a customer with a sweet Pomeranian that I made this mistake with once. They were Jewish, and her holiday colors are Blue and Silver. After that first year I made sure that I had Blue and Silver bows. I even went above and beyond and purchased a small Blue and Silver Plush Toy to send home as a gift the next year.

It is okay to make a mistake, the important part is to remember it, and not make the same mistake the following appointment.

Remember, you're there for the animals, but the owners pay the check.

TIP: Always visit the craft store AFTER the holiday to get all the discount deals on fabric and ribbon. A one-time purchase of a nice pair of fabric pinking shears will add some flair to your bandanas and help them not to fray.

There are plenty of how to videos on You Tube about how to make your own bows and bandanas if you are not familiar with doing it. I liked to sit down every so often in the evening when watching a movie and production line a bunch of bows and bandanas. If you work with multiple groomers in one salon you can have a team building exercise and share in the work.

If one of your customers expresses that they would prefer not to have bows or bandanas on their dog after a groom make sure you note that in their file and don't add those next time.

Listen to your clients.

We want to create both Remarkable Moments and Memorable Moments. And listening to them is an excellent way to create both.

Sending Cards

Last chapter we talked a bit about using the company Send Out Cards. Now let's talk about when you should send out a card to your clients. I didn't know about Send Out Cards when I was grooming, so I just purchased cards when they were on sale and had a stack of cards to choose from when I needed to send one out.

The point of sending these cards is to create a Memorable Moment, cause a Remarkable Moment, and stay top of mind with your clients.

Now that we are living in the Digital Age, not many people send, or get cards in the mail. Think of all the junk mail, bills, advertisements, etc. that you get in the mail on a weekly basis. Most of the time I don't even want to check my mailbox. Even Holiday cards are dwindling.

I am writing this on December 11th and I have yet to get one Holiday Card in the mail. How many of your clients live in assisted living homes? How often do they get cards from friends or family?

There is also a reason you want to send a card and not a Postcard. People have been trained since their childhood that junk-mail goes in the recycle bin, but a card, you open it, read it, and then put it on your desk, shelf, mantle, etc. People are trained to keep cards and throw away postcards. (unless they are travel postcards, but we're not grooming Fluffy on a beach in Costa Rica).

Send a Card

Send a Thank You card after a potential new clients' first groom.

When you find out a client is going in for surgery or is ill, send them a Get-Well card.

Be creative and send out a card for St. Patrick's Day, Groundhog Day, or New Year's card instead of Christmas or Hanukah.

Or send your personal holiday card to your clients too. They would love to see your family and your dogs.

Combine your Holiday card as a Reminder card about how busy the holiday season is, and to make sure to book their grooms early before you get booked up!

Send a card for the first day of Spring.

Send a card just to say hello.

Sympathy cards are the most important card you can send in my opinion. When you learn that one of your clients, their dog, or a family member passes away, take the time to hand write a card and send it in the mail. This means so much to them, shows that you care, and cements your relationship with them. You will be their groomer through multiple generations of dogs in their family.

Above and Beyond

Create a Memorable Moment by giving a gift or doing a prize giveaway drawing. I am hopelessly addicted to Shutterfly. You can create personalized items like coffee mugs, calendars, puzzles, photo books, ornaments, and so much more.

Since my daughter's birth I have made close to 10 (Free) Shutterfly photo books (Shhh, don't tell my Husband!). And she is only 3!

Gift a Photo Mug, or other inexpensive gift, to a client for their 1-year grooming anniversary. Remember your average client will pay you $435 per year, not including tips. This is an inexpensive and personal way to say Thank you for your business.

Create a Photo Calendar of some of your dog clients (get client permission first) and sell them to your customers with the profits going to a local dog charity. You get your work featured, your salon gets positive press, and you get to help a charity in need. Partner with the Charity so they can help market and sell the Calendars also. Cross promotion at its finest! Plus, your costs are covered by selling them.

Do a drawing one month where anyone who upgrades their grooming package gets put in a drawing for a prize giveaway. Get the prize donated by another company and it is no cost to you! I will discuss this more in the next chapter about Referral Partners and Networking.

Bark Cartons are another great way to create Memorable Moments. These are small folded food safe-cardstock boxes that you fill with treats and your business card. Give them away to clients who check in on your social media, give you a review, or to every 10th client as a surprise. You can also use them as a gift to your clients for referring new business to you.

People LOVE gifts and surprises!

There are so many ways to create a Memorable Moment. These were just a few examples, and the best part is they don't even have to be expensive, or cost money, they just have to be something special between you and your clients. You don't have to do them all, choose a few that you can start with and see how your clients react to them.

Creating Memorable Moments is an investment in your business and a distinct competitive advantage. It makes you stand out from your competition and builds strong relationships. No one can lure away a client who loves you. These loyal customers will be your raving fans, telling others about how great you are and become your own personal sales force.

By Kari Rouse

CHAPTER 8

Partnerships & Referral Partners

When I moved from Eugene back to the Portland area in Oregon it was very important to me to find a good Vet. At the time, I had a 120lb Rottweiler. There were two important things that I needed.

I wanted to make sure the Vet and their staff could handle a giant dog and not be afraid of him or have preconceived notions; he was a big sweetheart!

Since I had a lot of animal handling knowledge, I also wanted to be the one to hold him instead of a Vet Tech for standard blood draws and such.

After talking to my new co-workers and interviewing several Veterinarians I finally found the perfect one. Over the years we crafted such a great relationship. I also ended up getting a puppy Boston Terrier and she saw him from the beginning.

When I started grooming, I used this relationship I already had with my Vet and created a Referral Partnership. She had my business cards in her Office and when a client of hers asked about a good groomer in the area she sent them my way.

Remember Teddy the Westie from the beginning of the book? My Vet sent me that client!

When my clients asked me for a referral for a great Vet in the area, I gave them her business card and sent them her way.

That is what a great Referral Partnership looks like. It is mutually beneficial for both parties.

Earlier in this book we talked about ways for your clients to refer new business to you. In this chapter we will discuss the role of creating Partnerships with other businesses in the community and turning those partnerships into Referral Partners for your business.

I don't see Groomers taking advantage of this enough in my community.

A Partnership consists of doing an event together, like having a booth at the local farmers market or doggy 5k race.

Creating Co-branded Marketing Material where both of your business information together either in digital format, or paper format.

You could also create a partnership with a neighboring business and ask for something you can use as a FREE give-away. Create a beautiful display on your front desk and a sign about how to WIN it. Create the Rules for entry. Maybe your customers need to upgrade to the luxury service or send you a referral client in a specified time frame.

The ideas are limitless.

Partnerships can be created with other pet services businesses or with non-pet related businesses.

Creating a Referral Partnership takes the basic Partnership up a notch by actively referring business back and forth like in the example above with my Veterinarian.

In order to start this process for your business you will want to create a list and use the ICE method.

First thing you want to do is make a list of all the obvious businesses who serve your clientele. Those include Veterinarians, Dog Bakeries, the local Animal Shelter or Dog Rescue Organization, Dog Walkers/Sitters, Dog Poop Removal Company, Dog Photographers, Dog Kennel/Boarding Facility, Dog Rehab places, Dog Chiropractors... The list is endless.

Once you have a comprehensive list, you can then narrow down who you want to target first and start there.

Ice Method

An easy way to visually see where you should start is by using the ICE method. It is a type of business strategy and marketing strategy analysis.

ICE stands for:

I – Impact

C – Confidence

E – Effort

Let's make a chart. At the top put... Tactic – Impact – Confidence – Effort

Now under tactic put all your ideas for creating Partnerships. Just put them all down, good or bad.

Let's say your first Tactic is 'Create Partnership with Vet'. Maybe you have a great relationship with your Vet, so it would be easy to ask if you can partner with them and refer clients back and forth. You think this will have a major impact on your bottom line. Rate that an 8/10 for Impact.

You are confident that your assessment is correct, so your confidence is about a 7/10.

It will take minimal effort to start it, because you already have a relationship with your Vet, so all you need to do is ask, so the Effort is 3/10.

Now add the Impact + Confidence and subtract the Effort.

I + C – E = ICE

8 + 7 – 3 = 12

ICE = 12

Another example: Create a Partnership with a Dog Photographer.

You are not sure how much Impact creating a relationship with a Dog Photographer will have on your business, so you rate Impact at 4.

You are fairly confident that your assessment is correct, but you don't really know, so your confidence is about a 5/10.

You also don't currently know any Dog Photographers at the moment, so you will have to research that. The effort it will take to look them all up, call them, and try to meet with each one for a coffee to get to know each other's business... The effort on this one is 8/10.

I + C – E = ICE

4 + 5 – 8 = 1

Now let's review.

Create partnership with Vet: ICE = 12

Create partnership with Dog Photographer: ICE = 1

Now you can make an easy decision on which one to start with in your business. Do the task or tactic with the highest number because it's the one most likely to grow your business with the least effort.

You can also use this ICE strategy with other business marketing decisions. These could look like; 'consistently post on Facebook' or 'start an Instagram account' or 'send thank you cards to clients' or 'join a networking group' or 'hand out Bark Cartons at the dog park'...

Now that you have decided to go to your Vet to create a Referral Partnership, you can decide on what you have to offer the other person.

For example, you may choose to keep their cards in your shop so that when your clients ask about a good Vet in the area you can give them your Vet's card.

If you have an email list of your clients, you may choose to send out an email telling them about how great your Vet is.

In return, ask what the Vet is willing to do to send clients your way.

Remember, creating a stellar Referral Partnership is a two-way street and should put you both on equal footing.

Be realistic about your reach vs your potential partners reach. If your email list is 30 people and they have a list of 1000 people, that is not weighted as an equal Referral Partnership.

Here are a few other ideas to help boost each other's businesses and create a great Referral Partnership.

- You can send cross-promotions to the mailing list of each business.
- You can both mention cross promotions or share each other's social media posts.
- Take photos or videos and share them while at the other business.
- You can leave each other reviews about how great it is to work with them.

Bark Cartons as a Marketing Tool

Bark Cartons would be another great tool to use in your new Partnerships. Provide your Vet with boxes of treats including your business card to hand out to their clients as an added perk. The Vet looks good because they are handing out treats, and you get your name out to more people.

Another option to use Bark Cartons in this case is to Co-Brand your boxes. There are 4 available sides on the box, so you can have your information on 2 sides and the Vet can have thier information on 2 sides. Now you are splitting the cost of the boxes and reaching twice as many people.

As you build and add new Partnerships to your list, your joint Marketing efforts could look like this...

Next, partner with a Dog Bakery, who supplies the treats, adding their business card to the mix (or add them as another partner on your Bark Cartons). Now you have your name associated with the Vet's office and at the Dog Bakery as well!

When you Partner with the local Dog Walker, they can give out the Bakery's treats, the Vet's info, and your Grooming info! Your Bark Carton costs could be split 4 ways, and you are reaching not only new potential clients from your marketing efforts, but the marketing efforts of 3 other businesses as well.

The more Partnerships you create, the more you spread your name to new potential clients.

Bark Cartons can also be filled with your info and treats and given to the Gas Station across the street from you to pass out to the cars that fill up with dogs in the back seat.

You can do what Real Estate agents do and canvas whole neighborhoods with Bark Cartons (put them on door handles with a rubber band to drive new business to your salon). Choose the neighborhoods closest to your salon first and then strategically canvas the neighborhoods that fit your target demographic.

Check out this Blog Post for 50 ideas on how to use Bark Cartons as a Marketing Tool. www.barkcartons.com/50-ways-to-use-bark-cartons/

Once you have a good working relationship and have created Partnerships with the obvious dog related businesses in your area it is time to make a second list. This is a list of all the businesses who may not be directly related to your clients, or dog specific, but can still generate business and send it your way.

Get creative with your list, and remember, the worst that a potential Partnership business can tell you is, No.

Maybe approach the hardware store that allows dogs to shop with their owners. They could hand a Bark Carton box with your info and treats to every paying customer with a dog.

People who love dogs often go walking or hiking, so try partnering with a local shoe store.

What about the coffee shop who has a dog water dish outside their store?

Usually Apartment Complexes give move-in packages to new residents that move into the community. A move-in pack contains coupons and menus and such for local businesses. Apartment complexes give these to all the people who move in so that they can easily find the local services they need. Why not go and speak with the manager of the Apartment down the street from your shop to see if you can add your information to their Welcome Packet?

Is your business in a complex with other businesses? Maybe you can speak with the other owners of the business and work some kind of cross promotion out? Example: Dinner and a Groom. The Diner next door offers a coupon for dinner while you offer a discount on services while your customers dine.

Or a Movie and Groom night. (Same thing with a Movie Theater).

There are even Real Estate Agents who call themselves "pet-friendly real estate agents". Make a connection with a local agent. When they have new buyers moving into the area who own dogs, they can refer them to you for grooming.

There are so many options to consider, just choose a few to start with and go from there. Creating Partnerships and Referral Partners WILL increase your business. Studies have shown that customers who are referred to you, stay longer, spend more, complain less, and themselves are twice as likely to refer others. Those are the kinds of clients you need!

Remember, once you establish these relationships you need to nurture them, just like you do with your own clients. Don't set up a Partnership and never speak to them again. Check in on them often, surprise them with a card, and try to send your clients their way also.

You will be top of mind when it is time for them to refer a great groomer.

By Kari Rouse

CHAPTER 9

Networking

Networking is yet another thing I don't see Groomers, or pet industry people in general, taking advantage of. I think it is because we just don't realize it is out there, and/or that it isn't right for us. In the past 5 years that I have been networking I have only met ONE pet-businessperson, who was a dog walker, and she never came back!

What is networking?

> *net·work*
>
> */ˈnetˌwərk/*
>
> *verb*
>
> *connect as or operate with a network.*
>
> *"the stock exchanges have proven to be resourceful in networking these deals"*
>
> *link (machines, especially computers) to operate interactively.*
>
> ***interact with other people to exchange information and develop contacts, especially to further one's career.***
>
> *"the skills of networking, bargaining, and negotiation"*

At a fundamental level, networking is meeting more people than you know now. That's really the basis of it, to know more people.

Business Networking consists of a group of professionals from various backgrounds and industries. They get together on a weekly, bi-monthly, or monthly basis (depending on the group) to mingle, create professional relationships, and to pass referrals. You get a chance to give your elevator pitch (more on this later), hand out business cards, and learn about other businesses in your area.

Over the last several years I have been to many different Networking groups and I have grown more confident as a person and business owner by attending on a regular basis.

This is a HUGE resource that is vastly underutilized in the Pet Services industry! Some businesses get as much as half of their business from networking groups alone. Are you missing out on half of your potential business?

Farming vs. Hunting

Think about Networking as a farming activity instead of a hunting activity. Each week you tend the soil, sow the seeds, and water them. Over the course of the season you can watch your seeds grow into plants. Only when your plants are ripe will you be able to harvest your crop.

You know it takes time to build trust and relationships with your customers. It also takes time to build relationships in the business world and only then do you see the benefit of referral clients walking in your door.

Too many times I have witnessed and been on the receiving end of someone trying to use Networking as a Hunting opportunity.

When you go with the sole intention of shoving as many business cards as possible into people's hands, and only talk about you and your business trying to turn everyone into money walking through your door, it is painfully obvious to everyone at the event.

Please don't go into these meetings to hunt your prey and drag them back to your business. It comes off as disingenuous, and really puts off people who are in Networking for the long haul.

Basically, Networking is stepping out of your comfort zone to go meet professional business people, like yourself. People who have money, usually own or manage businesses, and most likely, a lot of them have dogs, even if they don't, they know people who do.

Benefits of Networking

There are many benefits to having a good Networking practice. One of the main benefits is the huge potential of creating great Referral Partnerships. In the last chapter we focused on how to create Referral Partners.

Every networking group usually has at least one Real Estate Agent. They know who is moving in and out of the area. They know if their clients have dogs/cats. Since they are trusted by their clients, they are in the perfect position to refer your services. Maybe you can even get some branded treats, flyers, or Bark Carton added to their Move-in gift.

But you have to make that connection first. That is where networking comes into play.

Depending on your Target Market, another great referral partner could be the Manager to a Senior Living Center, or the Manager of a new Apartment Building. There are so many great businesses represented at these networking groups.

The point is, you stay top of mind with people through networking. These people are well connected in the community. When the need arises for your services, your business with be the first mentioned.

It's like magic!

Another benefit of Networking with other Professional Businesspeople is that you are all running businesses. This means that if you have a business-related issue, like where to get help with your books, payroll, or tenant/landlord issues, you have someone you already know and trust to help mentor you or point you in the right direction.

You are not alone in the business world.

One of the biggest benefits that I received from repeatedly going to Networking Groups is a boost in my confidence. At first, I found it to be a bit overwhelming and I did not like public speaking at all. But over time I was able to refine my elevator pitch and started to feel more comfortable and confident when speaking in front of people.

Start by checking out your local Chamber of Commerce.

Not only do they usually hold regular Networking Meetings, but they have a huge amount of resources for local businesses too.

My local chamber hosts an event called "Wake Up!" every Friday Morning from 8 am to 9 am at a different local business each week. Most Chambers of Commerce will allow you to visit their meetings a couple of times for free without having to join so that you can check it out.

It is important to note that your local chamber of commerce is not the same organization as the National Chamber of Commerce. The U.S. Chamber of Commerce is not a governing body or regulatory agency for other state, county, or city chambers.

Any community can organize and support a chamber of commerce and there may be multiple ones in different cities. Some may be industry-specific, like the "Health and Wellness Chamber of Commerce" or for a specific part of a city like the "North AnyTown Chamber of Commerce." That means every Chamber is going to be a little different, so you want to visit and see what they have to offer.

Other Groups

I have also visited BNI (Business Networking International), LeTip, NetPerking, groups I have found on MeetUp, and any other group in my area that starts up. Each group is different, has a different cost, time commitment, and feel. I am now a member (and President) of 2 Womens Only groups called WIN (Women in Networking).

You usually get to visit each group 2 or 3 times without paying for a membership (if there is a cost) so you can check out almost any networking group for free.

I suggest you visit as many groups as you can until you find one that fits your needs. Once in, take the time to get to know the members, use their services, refer them to your clients, and you will find you will start to get referrals from them as well.

Why should you stick with Networking for the long haul?

Just like building client relationships is based on the know, like, and trust model that builds over time, business Networking relationships grow in a similar way. Follow a few simple steps to start building real business relationships.

Show up to meetings on-time.

Introduce yourself to people and ask them what they do... then LISTEN.

Ask questions about what they do and learn from them.

If they ask about you and your business, give them your elevator pitch (we'll talk about that soon), then answer any questions they have, and then ask them more questions. **This is about THEM, it's not about you.**

It's OK to ask them about their pets, but they will usually volunteer that information. Talk to them about your pets.

Find common ground and interests.

Woah! Wait a minute, this sounds like making friends. Surprise! That's what you're doing.

You can't build these relationships by going to just one or two meetings or showing up without consistency. The real magic starts to happen, and referrals start to call and walk through your door when you establish a meaningful connection.

What are meeting generally like?

Meetings can vary widely from group to group, and what type of event you are attending. As stated above, over the years I have been to several different types of events, and while they do have different rules within each group there are some basic consistencies as well.

First, make sure you bring enough business cards for the type of event you are attending. Ask the membership coordinator or person who invited you ahead of time what you should expect.

Some of the smaller groups you go to expect to bring 20 cards or so, but there are also mega events like Speed Networking where you literally meet 100 people and exchange business cards in timed 1-minute increments.

The purpose of going to each of these events is different. For example, the smaller groups usually have a membership requirement where you go on a weekly basis and attendance is tracked.

You create relationships with all members who then refer you out to others when they are at other networking groups and in daily life.

The larger events are more for finding a business to fill a specific need of yours. Go into one of these events with the intention of meeting 2-3 specific people.

Example: You need to find a bookkeeper for your business, or you want to make a key partnership with a Real Estate Agent, or if you are a house sitter you want to meet a Travel Agent so they can refer their clients to you while they go on vacation.

Once you have made those specific introductions and have their business cards then you will need to contact them to schedule a one on one meeting for coffee/tea to get to know each other better and hammer out the specifics of possibly creating a mutually beneficial partnership.

If you get stuck and not sure what to talk about in a *One-to-One,* simply remember FORD. Family, Occupation, Recreation, and Dreams. A conversation could potentially look like this...

"Are you married/have kids? Tell me about that."

"What do you love about what you do for a living?"

"What do you do for fun on the weekends?"

"Do you have any big plans for this ear/summer?"

It should be casual. You are getting to know each other.

Most meetings have an introduction phase where you will often get the opportunity to give your one-minute elevator pitch. Talk about what you do, your target clients, and what sets you apart from your competition. What are the benefits your clients see, and what benefits do referral partners get when they partner with you?

Basically, why are you awesome, and how do you stand above your competition.

Then depending on the group, you may hear a member presentation about their business. Listen and ask questions if you have them.

Finally, groups tend to wrap up with some kind of 'Thank you's', or Closed Business discussion, or Business Wins.

Make sure that if you have a chance to speak at this point to Thank the presenter and the group for having you there. And tell them you are looking forward to getting to know them better. You usually have time before or after the meeting to set up some one on ones with people you want to get to know better. Don't get overwhelmed, start small and build each week. Set aside time to create these relationships.

Here are my top 5 tips for networking.

Go in with confidence. You are a professional!

Bring a ton of business cards. Don't just hand them out to everyone, but when someone asks for one you will have them on hand.

At many groups, such as BNI, they often allow visitors to pass their business cards around the group. My husband's BNI group that he attends has more than 35 members, so you need to make sure you have a LOT of cards.

Don’t go in expecting to make a sale right away. Go in with the intention of creating connections and new relationships.

Wear something that makes you stand out and be memorable.

Consistency is key. Don’t give up, keep going. Believe me, all this hard work will pay off in the long run!

Welcome to the big leagues, Networking Pro! And remember, you will get better at this over time. You don’t have to be perfect to start.

CHAPTER 10

Social Media

Social Media is a huge opportunity to grow your business. Before social media we strictly had to rely on word of mouth, or some other kind of print material getting in front of our new potential customers. Television and Radio were/are another option, but most groom shops, except for national chains, can't afford these types of mass media marketing.

Today we can simply post a picture or a story to Facebook or Instagram and have it shared to many potential customers around your area with little footwork on your part.

Or can you?

We'll talk more about this in a minute.

I won't go into it here, but you should also have a simple website (a micro site is sufficient) as well as your social media pages. This is a place for your potential customers to find out specific information about you and your business, like address, phone number, and your background.

If you are employed by one of the big box stores, you probably won't have the need for a website, except to establish your own personal brand. But it is still a great idea to maintain and upkeep your social media channels.

Remember, you are establishing YOU as your BRAND. If you ever go to another shop or move to another location you will still have your website and social media accounts to establish your history and as a portfolio of your work.

I rarely see someone use these platforms to their greatest potential. It is easy for a groomer to simply take before and after pictures of their client's dogs showing the magical transformation from dirty and stinky to perfectly groomed masterpiece. But seriously, how many people want to see photo after photo (all day long) of grooms?

We LIVE the #GroomerLife, our customers don't.

What are your customers interested in? Sure, they are interested in seeing that you can groom. Having a portfolio is a must. But that isn't going to keep your audience following you. Instead, think about what they want to see. What would they like and/or share?

I encourage you to become the expert on all things dog in your area. Go and take photos and/or video at all the local dog parks. Report back if they are muddy or well kept. (Hint: while you are there you can hand out dog treats in Bark Cartons with your business cards!) Double Whammy!!

Visit Coffee shops who allow dogs to sip Pupachinnos with their owners and tell your audience about your favorite coffee in the shop.

Do you have local walking or hiking trails? Take your dog and take photos/video along the way.

Are you involved with doing charity grooms at the local Shelter? Showcase each shelter dog in a video and tell their story. The finally of the video can be your haircut and that 'Fluffy' is now ready for his forever home. This content will get shared out and

'Fluffy' will find his home faster than if he wasn't featured in your video. (You can also leave a hand-written card with your business card for the new owners letting them know you would love to groom their new family member).

The possibilities here are endless! Find what your audience resonates with and go with it. Post more of what they like and share, and less of the other stuff.

Try starting with this list of ideas:

1. Video of different combs/brushes that your clients would need for at home maintenance.
2. Video on how to properly brush out their dog.
3. What to look for when an ear has an infection and needs to be seen by their vet.
4. You could do a series of breed profiles talking about the pros and cons of each breed and what maintenance, exercise, activity, space they need.
5. How to handle a puppies' feet so they get used to that for grooming and nail trims.
6. A day in the life of a groomer. Behind the scenes fun in the grooming shop.
7. Highlight client dogs of the week/month (with owner consent) and talk about how awesome they are.
8. A report of conditions at the local dog park.

9. A glimpse into what your life is like outside of the grooming salon. Do you like to hike, garden, have a family, own your own pets, etc...
10. Updated news for your area about flea/tick season, rabid animal sightings, safety info.
11. What medicine you recommend to control fleas/ticks for prevention.
12. Highlight other businesses you love (these will be your partnerships/referral partners), and why you love them.
13. Talk about any continuing education you are working on.
14. Talk about a charity you love to work with.
15. Rescue animals needing forever homes.
16. Your company specials. (Follow the 80/20 rule. It states that 80% of your social media posts should fall under 3 categories. Inform, Educate, and Entertain. 20% will be your company's promotions.)

There are so many ideas out there.

Make it fun, make it interesting.

Remember what we talked about back in Chapter 3 about Remarkable Content. Content that people make a Remark about.

When you position yourself as the expert on everything dog in your community you will see your following not only grow, but also become more responsive to what you post.

Social media platforms want people to stay on their apps and websites longer. They reward content that you make that people like, comment on, share, watch longer, etc.

When you make things that your customers and potential customers are interested in, it makes them engage more, and the social media platforms will reward you by showing your posts to more people.

That improved "reach" you get by posting things that get people to tap the "like" button is free advertising for you!

By Kari Rouse

CHAPTER 11

Marketing Ideas

You're busy. And like most businesspeople, you have fallen into the trap of only working in your business and never working on your business.

We have already talked about marketing ideas throughout the book and in this section, we're going to talk about implementing them. Ideas are great, but if you don't act, ideas aren't going to make you more money.

Because each of you is in a different place in your business, select the ideas that can best help your business grow. Set aside time to accomplish these things. Gary Kellar, author of "The One Thing" and a literal billionaire said in an interview (and I am paraphrasing here), "Setting aside time to work on your business is like putting a rock in a stream. The work will flow around it like water. So, guard your time."

Create a Website

There are many website builders out there or local agencies who can help you design a website. Keep it simple. If you have a website, go over every page and make sure it's up to date. If you don't know how to update it, find a local freelancer or agency who can assist you. Remember to keep those receipts, because your website and website updates are a write-off on your income for tax purposes.

Other To-Do's

- Set up your Schedule/Calendar
- Create time for you to work on your business.
- Block out your networking time.
- Schedule the time to write your newsletter/blog/social media content.
- Stick to your calendar.
- Create your Social Media Accounts
- Both Facebook and Instagram have the option to create a business account with phone number, address, website...
- Research and attend a Networking Group or two
- For more in-depth information on Networking consult Chapter 9.
- Make a list of all past clients and potential clients and write them a letter telling them of your new venture/move coming up.
- Create Partnerships with businesses in your area
- For more in-depth information about creating Partnerships consult Chapter 8.

- Create a Marketing Calendar for the next 6 months – year
- This consists of all the Marketing tasks you want to do on a daily/monthly/quarterly basis within your marketing. You can find free templates online.
- Once a month Schedule an Outside the box idea (Shelter video, visit dog parks, local dog-friendly hikes)
- Create a Customer Avatar
- This is a more in-depth look at who your target client is. You give them a name, age, likes/dislikes, income level, activities/hobbies... Use this Avatar when you are writing your marketing copy so they feel like you are speaking directly to them. Customer Avatar Worksheet in the Appendix.
- Check Out the Competition
- What services do they offer?
- What are their prices like?
- How do they go above and beyond for their clients?
- Engage with Your Local Chamber of Commerce
- You will find a wealth of small business help and information at your local Chamber of Commerce.
- This is also a great place to network and meet other business owners in your community.
- Add a Follow-Up Process

- What do you currently do to follow up with your clients? For more information on follow-up, consult Chapter 6.

Become Locally Famous

Just 3 short years ago, I didn't know almost any of the businesspeople I know now. You want to become well known in your area by...

- Showing up to the Networking events.
- Make Partnerships with key businesses in your community.
- Review and share other people's content, and when you create your own content that people want to see, those partners will share your content as well.

Your name will be the first to mind when someone gets a new dog or moves into the area.

"Oh, you NEED to take Fido to see Groomer Kari, she is AMAZING!"

When you have an army of ambassadors for your brand you will reap the benefits of all that referral business.

This is a long-game mindset. You aren't going to take an action once and expect business to fall into your lap. Every week you need to be strategically implementing and executing your strategy so that in the long run your work will pay off.

This reminds me of the cartoon/meme that periodically goes around on social media where the two people are digging for gold and it shows one about to strike it rich and another who gave up, a few shovels-full of dirt away from striking gold.

Don't stop just before you reach the gold.

Remember Client Lifetime Value that we talked about at the beginning of the book?

When you are paying for marketing you aren't just trading your marketing budget for that $50 for the initial groom. You are going for the client lifetime value of $1305.

Make sure when new clients come in you ask them where they heard of you. You want to keep a record of this and track what is working and what isn't working for bringing in new clients.

Make sure you review this every month and adjust your marketing efforts based on the success you've found so far. If something is bringing in more paying clients, do that more.

In order to keep track of your numbers from week to week and month to month, you can use a simple excel spread sheet. Track things like your social media following. Your promotions going on and how many customers you are bringing in with each marketing campaign. Make sure you also track your email subscribers and keep trying to get more people on your list.

These should be tracked in addition to your weekly/monthly revenue goals, and/or pet counts. Without keeping track of the numbers, you have no idea if you are growing your business or staying stagnant in relation to the additional effort you are expending.

You have to take action.

Take action now!

Write down some ideas or highlight them in the book and put a bookmark on this chapter.

None of this will help grow your business if you don't take the ideas and put them into practice. If you use just a few of the strategies in this book, you will start to grow your business and your status as a member of the business community.

CHAPTER 12

Conclusion

My research and experience in the Dog Grooming landscape has shown me that Grooming Professionals and animal service providers, in general, are on the outskirts of the 'Professional' Business realm. You deserve to be taken seriously in the business marketplace, and by your customers.

In writing this book and launching Bark Cartons my intentions are to help you step up into your role as experts in your industry. Stop having clients try to haggle about prices with you (nobody tries to argue with the mechanic, plumber or human hairdresser about their service prices).

You are highly talented, intuitive, and passionate.

You deserve to be treated with respect and dignity!

You also deserve to be paid a decent and fair rate for the hard work you do. Please don't sell yourself short! Slashing prices or giving huge discounts with the hopes to attract a clientele is a race to the bottom. Not only is it unsustainable, but it cheapens your service, and the grooming profession.

Stand out by giving excellent customer service and creating Memorable Moments for your clients.

Businesses who give better service, have better follow-up, pre-book clients, and differentiate themselves have clients who pay more, stay longer, and complain less. Trust me, everyone will be happier in the end.

Know that no matter if you are grooming under the umbrella of a big box store, or a private salon, you are entitled to be treated with respect. If you are not feeling appreciated, are constantly harassed, or told that you aren't good enough, you don't have to justify finding somewhere else that is a better fit. I want you to know that you deserve much better.

In hindsight, I should have quite my job at the big box store much, much sooner and started my own grooming business. Who knows, I may still be grooming if I had, but that topic is for another book.

During my grooming career I lead many different teams at several different salons. Each salon increased their sales and built their businesses so that they were making a profit each week, but as soon as I moved on, every salon dropped in sales again.

The problem is personal motivation. When I taught these tools to each groomer, they either implemented them, or ignored them. When you ignore them, you are essentially just waiting for business to fall into your lap.

And you better hope another shop doesn't open up down the street with this book in their pocket.

You are using the Pray method. Praying that business will call or walk in your door. Using this method, you will see seasonal dips, slow times, and you will not have a steady paycheck.

Don't be average.

Stand out from the crowd.

Give excellent customer service.

Create Memorable Moments with each client who walks through your door.

Watch your clientele grow.

Reap the Benefits of your hard work!

I have grown groom shops and profitable businesses using these strategies. You work hard, and you deserve to be rewarded. There is a wonderful feeling of accomplishment that comes with growing your business and there is a peace that comes with knowing your bills are paid and your clients will keep coming back.

My sincere hope is for you to take the information from this book, implement it into your business, and grow your profits and your happiness this year and many more to come.

In the end, the animals you serve will come out as the winners.

By Kari Rouse

APPENDIX

Visit www.BarkCartons.com

For more marketing resources and information visit Bark Cartons.

Browse the pre-made Bark Carton designs or create your own custom box by contacting me directly.

The Bark Marketing Collective

Join in the discussion at The Bark Marketing Collective, a group of Pet Services professionals like yourself who are working together to build their own pet empires.

Running your own business can get lonely at times. Get peer support, celebrate your WINS, work through your hardships, and get marketing support. Structured learning material added to the learning section regularly.

This is also a resource to create partnerships with other pet professionals in your area.

Customer Avatar Worksheet

Remember, you want to get as detailed as possible in this step of the process. The more you know about your customer, the easier it is to directly market to them and attract new clients.

PRODUCT/SERVICE: ________________ DATE:

____

NAME: Name your client. This will help to connect you to the avatar and you can speak directly to them when you are writing your marketing copy. My avatar is named Jane.

DEMOGRAPHICS

GENDER: LOCATION[S]:
MARITAL STATUS: AGE RANGE: # OF KIDS:

Are they married? How old are they? Do they have children? Where do they live? What kind of lifestyle do they have?

KNOW YOUR CUSTOMER

WHAT ARE THEIR PERSONAL GOALS AND CHALLENGES?

GOALS: What goals do they have?

Do they want to go on a vacation every year?

Do they want to advance in their career?

Do they participate in some kind of sport or activity?

VALUES: What do they value?

Do they support local?

Do they purchase high quality brands? Do they value integrity and honesty?

CHALLENGES: What challenges do they face on a daily/weekly/monthly basis?

Do they struggle to pay their bills, or do they live comfortably?

Do they have a hard time keeping up with the tasks they set on their calendar?

PAIN POINTS: What causes them pain?

What do they fear?

Could be that they fear being judged by their peers, or fear they don't have enough time to accomplish what they want to achieve in life...

WHERE THEY GO What activities do they do?

What organizations are they involved in? Where can you find them?

WHERE DO THEY GET THEIR INFORMATION?

SITES FOR RESEARCH: Do they Google information?

Have a favorite website?

SITES FOR DIY: Do they use Pinterest or other Do It Yourself websites?

SITES FOR ENTERTAINMENT: What do they watch on TV?

What kind of movies do they watch?

What hobbies do they participate in?

WHERE DO THEY GET NEWS: TV station?

Website?

Friends?

Work?

Facebook?

BOOKS/MAGAZINES: What do they read?

On-line, or in print?

OTHER:

PURCHASE & SALES

WHO IS THE DECISION MAKER AND WHAT SHOULD WE KNOW? Do they make the decisions in their household?

Or do they have a spouse who makes the decisions?

How does this relationship work?

WHO IS THE FINAL DECISION MAKER: Who makes the final decision?

Is it a partnership, or does one person need permission?

ROLE IN DECISION PROCESS: How is the final decision made?

OBJECTIONS TO PURCHASE: What are the potential objections to purchasing your service?

Is it Cost?

If the dog is matted, maybe an objection is that the final haircut is too short.

TRUST IN PURCHASE: Trust is a huge factor in the final purchase. They must trust your expertise. Use this section to overcome any objections brought up in the previous section. That way when they come up, you have something prepared to say in response.

How do they know they have made the best decision in the end?

Start Now

Spend some time on this and make it as detailed as you can. The more you know about your potential client, the better.

Once you know who you are targeting you can make sure your copy on your website, social media, and print material matches who you are wanting to attract.

Scenario One: You advertise you're the cheapest in town and hand out coupons.

In this scenario, you are basically trying to get anyone who has a dog to come into your business.

Now let's try another approach.

Scenario Two: You fill out the customer avatar worksheet. You decide to look for customers who are interested in having a relationship with you and don't mind spending more money for better service.

You are looking for someone who is financially stable and wants to schedule monthly grooming. They are also someone who likes to buy high quality products and loves the convenience of having a standing appointment each month without having to think about it.

An advertisement or sales letter for people who fit this avatar worksheet would look something like this:

Do you have every minute of the day scheduled?

When you have to run your kids to 3 different sporting events on the same day, plus get work done, you don't have time to research a new groomer every month.

Keep Fido looking his best every month at The Dog Spa.

You can trust that Fido will feel pampered and come home looking his best.

We use top of the line products and have years of animal care experience.

You deserve to have the best.

Become part of our pet family today and save some time for your busy schedule in the process.

You aren't going to advertise that you are the cheapest groomer in town.

Do you see what the difference is there?

That customer isn't looking for the cheapest. They are looking for high quality, professional services.

They are going to want to be treated as such and enjoy the extra services you offer. They want the convenience of a pre-booked appointment, and the relationship they are going to build with you over the long run.

Conclusion

These two scenarios above are targeting two very different client groups. In the top example you are inviting the bargain shopper who just looks for the cheapest groom and hops from shop to shop each month based on price.

This is NOT the client you want to attract for long term growth and profitability.

The second scenario is inviting someone who wants to create a long-term relationship with you. Someone who cares about quality. This client enjoys the ease of using your services every month because it is one less thing they must think about in their daily lives.

Fill your books with these clients and you will have a steady business you can be proud of.

By Kari Rouse

I would love to hear from you!

Visit www.BarkCartons.com

For more marketing resources and information visit BarkCartons.com and we can carry on the conversation from there!

Happy Grooming!

~Kari Rouse

www.ingramcontent.com/pod-product-compliance
Lightning Source LLC
Chambersburg PA
CBHW021836170526
45157CB00007B/2812
* 9 7 8 1 0 7 5 7 5 2 9 6 4 *